ORANGE FANTA

ORANGE FANTA

CHARLES ELIN

ARPress
ILLUMINATING IDEAS.
EMPOWERING VOICES.

ARPress
45 Dan Road Suite 36
Canton MA 02021

Hotline: 1(888) 821-0229
Fax: 1(508) 545-7580

Ordering Information:
Quantity Sales. Special discounts are available on quantity purchases by corporations, associations, and others. For details, contact the publisher at the address above.

Printed in the United States of America.

ISBN-13   Paperback   979-8-89330-749-8
                eBook   979-8-89330-750-4

Library of Congress Control Number: 2024902890

ACKNOWLEDGEMENTS

BoomerLitMag: *Morning Pine*
The Borfski Press: *Gripping the Ash*
California Quarterly: *The World in Four Lines*
Chantwood Magazine: *Eyes of the Soil* and *His Brain on Blue*
Forge: *Orange Fanta*
The Griffin: *Piano Ash*
The Lindenwood Review: *Something to Hold on to*
Mantis: *Hand Art*
Short Edition: *Marnie*
SLAB: *North Country*
The Slag Review: *and now for something good*
The Round: *Scientific American*

To Mimi
who is there in every poem

TABLE OF CONTENTS

MORNING PINE

The still lake throws back a forest,
blurred beyond recognition. As a boy,
he did something and walked into
a family myth. He's reminded of
the latest version as words pile on.
The loons called last night. They left
only vowels, in no hurry for a used story.

THE RELATION OF A THOUSAND PIECES

Self-deception was never possible. He heard otherwise,
but couldn't find its whereabouts. He was bound by skin.
There, underneath, he heard was the underlying. He went about
his business. It was so close to real. If memory served, he
knew his name. Beyond that there were pieces. Resembling
all he never lost.

THE COLLAPSE OF KNOWING

In the order of things, he took a walk.
The trees were upright. Sticks were on the ground.
His heart pounded, sweat poured. Anything was possible.
A falling was in the air. His partner never showed.
And even so, there were things not to mention.
Predicates were in the brush. His eyes watered.

SILK

The spider flew as it let out silk. No one noticed
the warm air rising. He took a dive into energy.
None of the fanfare came his way. His parents
were there from the beginning. They heard the noise.
His scream shook the cord. He was ready to be a bother.

SCIENTIFIC AMERICAN

As a toddler, he didn't talk. Playing, too,
was a mystery. Things on the floor looked
like his mind. An army of green, with hard-to-see
weapons. When older, he studied cellular identity
and bought a home. His wife wanted her own room.
And there was no compromising.

MAKING FLUFF

Fluffy the doodle. The end.
And now she's on to something else.
The dog has a mind of its own.
His head points. Not to be fooled with.
Her Pa defined a dog. It didn't work.
He created a bystander. The fear was
in losing Democracy. Just as the self
became a word. His friends were busy
playing on the ground.

VERY

He calls her by the adverb.
So much of growing is
growing. The first time
all over again. Very good.
Very big girl. Now, she teaches.
If not here, then go back where
you came from. Distance is no
object. They know in advance.
Repetition. Repetition. We all
need a practice range. The country
sweeps and sweeps. All those
spent casings.

ORANGE FANTA

for the late Larry Fagin

Effervescence, had he thought of it. Out of the common can. By way of
Creeley, Beckett reports. One word. May that be the extent of language. A
bubble with benefits. Relations rising. It was quite a ride.

His peas run into the Bolognese. An offense worth noting. Each, of its own
character. He'd place himself in the audience. Embarrassed for the actor,
caught acting.

THE BATTLE OF OUTSIDE AND INSIDE

The man with one short leg learned from the beginning.
Some were frightened. Others fearful. He looked
straight ahead. Eye contact was an outside activity.
Inside, he smiled. His face was stiff, unbending.
He could see through others. Up against the wall.

MARNIE

Marnie liked melodies. In her city room facing nowhere, the routine was the same. At night, she sang naked out the open window. It was a way to get inside. A chorus, she thought, might feel the same. If only she knew the half of it. It was the harmony that got in the way. She felt it disorienting. It made her nauseous. *Singing acapella is the height of pleasure*, she heard how many times. Normality must be a joint sensation. And yet, her body had another idea. Marnie became physically excited by the blending of sounds. It happened during rehearsals and performances. Soon it brought her to orgasm, which made her feel ashamed. She learned to hide her condition in the raised volume of the chorus. One evening, on the subway ride home, Marnie hung onto a pole during a sharp turn. After another jolt, she grabbed it again. This time her hand wrapped around the hand of another woman. Both women left their hands in place as the train completed the bend and eased into the next station. The stranger got off at her stop without looking back.

THE OUTHOUSE

What he needs is more land. And a portable outhouse.
Hidden behind the trees. It happens all the time.
The urge to use is proportional to what's available.
He'll be fine. Waiting is a virtue. Not feeling the wait,
even better. He began to pay bills. The car was his, now.
He drove cross country for a visit. No one was home.
So he drove back. Forget the outhouse, he thought.

GRIPPING THE ASH

Books beat in his head, a drifter with a pulse.
He was a witness. Food being charred.
Letting it go made all the difference.
There was a movement. Then a counter-movement.
He had a spot off to the side—watching democracy.
Death is so sudden. A quick burn. Online he found the boots.
All the marchers had them.

REGULARS

He knew how, with a smile and a sign. A woman apologized
for not having change. It was a busy sidewalk. The man behind
her was a regular. She watched as he parted with his dollar.
She, too, was a regular. Her legs moved, as did his. Being next
to each other, they were together. Some regulars have this understanding.
Then, it happened. In a block he said good-bye, turning the corner.
It didn't seem possible. This was a man who would be by her side.
It was a parting before history could push back.

HAND ART

The potter sold with her hands. Long sweeping strokes. He
thought it was
all a muddle. It's not for me, he said, losing control of his words.
His eye
was on the potter. He should buy something. A small piece to
move around.
The potter's long neck rode into her arm and off into thin air.
I'd like to buy
your hand, he said. The potter once had a dog. She used to pull
him close
and shout in-between the eyes: Who's in there?
She thought about this and took her time.

TIMES NEW ROMAN

She can't find the sheet. He suggests her pocketbook.
Things go missing. She's reminded of the beauty parlor,
forced to listen to the hair down. She holds onto
her things, watching what she can't bear. Under oath,
would anything be different? She nods off, interrogated
by men in helmets.

MONOLOGUES

No one voted today. The weight of location,
far from the maddening crowds. She talked to herself
when with others. The divide, now an institutional cult.
She never knew herself as more than expected.
The moving pictures of a mass grave filled the screen.
She watched as each was tossed.

OUT OF SIGHT

She's not serious about drain control. Plastic pieces scoot their way
into the disposal unit. Rubber bands hiss. This is why the back
of her head
doesn't matter. They argued about tattoos. She wanted one down
her arm.
He preferred something out of sight. Her sight. The eyes can be
a distraction,
he thought.

How far back is motivation? He looked at his watch. Scarred
with childhood
impressions, he went to the store. There were things to grab.
Genetically,
he comes from a long line. He wanted that for her. There was
no payment.

THERE, THE SAME

She couldn't describe the chair. Her muscle was the problem. It was easier to reference the pain. As a grandma, she walked pretty-well. Green and purple flowers lined the path. Her granddaughter noticed. Same as my shoes, Grandma.

From four to fourteen is a big jump. The best we know, she said, is to describe. With a telescope, there were animals living alongside the infinite. She saw the sand as the same. No one noticed her digging. The parking lot was hot. A convertible was baking. She walked with her pail and dumped it. Right in the front seat. That night the sky was there, still in alignment. She closed her eyes and fell asleep. It was like being awake. She got married as herself as her grandma.

CRIB AND CRIB

She really, really liked her crib. Sure she grew out of it,
but not her affection. When older and single she got back in.
She knew this carpenter. He built her one to fit. In pregnancy,
she had more decisions. Would she get a second crib or share
the big one? She had nightmares about crushing the baby.
It was too much to think about. They slept in separate cribs.
Soon the baby became the adult. She drove to the nursing home
every night. Her mom wanted to be tucked in. The bed came with
railings.

DENTAL WORK

His teeth were in the way. Tapping, once outside of
attention. There were places to mark. A small bite
when passing a sign. Then, just to feel it again. His jaw
was looking for old times, the way a woman can sit.
And toggle her leg in public. His tongue got into the act.
Behind the scenes of his own film. Close-up thoughts,
trying to get away. There were clear titles below the action.
While driving in a foreign land. It was a movie not yet made.
Talking no more than the translation. Not to get ahead of those
catching up on the pace of real speech.

AND NOW FOR SOMETHING GOOD

They think he's nervous, watching him flirt
with what once was, never too far from the porch.
Joy aside, it's not what he wanted to say,
in re-emerging so weathered. A family grows
in the time it takes to consider.

GAINING ON CLARITY

He planned it all falling asleep.
Running into something.
He knew what to do.
The simplest of ideas.
Like the day. Hours spent.
When a darkness creeps in.
Too late to be. Whatever, they say.

NORTH COUNTRY

inspired by the artwork of Al Chasan

So many colors in a dying sun.
Insects, the last to find water,
shelter deep in the bark.
Mutations are under way.
Biology braces for its promise
of a melting pot.

HIS BRAIN ON BLUE

inspired by the artwork of Al Chasan

It's not a tracing. Lines creep into folds,
where a movement drops by. The unknown
was thought to be black. He pointed his
brush at the slow burn and let it ride.
Marching, slouching toward Bethlehem.
The sky's reflection is the only ground

PIANO ASH

Notes drop light
on dust, moving the
still air. Dead space
laughing, crawls under
stair lip, never find
the picture framed in
shadow

EYES OF THE SOIL

Anything but a poem. An anger, well-placed needs no confined spacing. That it is not one, caught in some human condition. How far we've come, looking into the eyes—when forced to take a stand. The country picks at its wounds and we take a step back. Judges were once healers; oversight, a remedy. Let the final tool be used to dig up memos.

SOMETHING TO HOLD ON TO

The wrapping was homemade. A long-handle coffee measure. Perfect for
his 75th. At 85, the options were challenging. It was the day of his death.
They all knew it. There was nothing left to use. He knew it too.
His birthday was today. There were murmurs. He wanted to join the party.
"Presents," he whispered, when he meant "present." He was remembering
his 75th and was still thankful. They thought he wanted more.

THE WORLD IN FOUR LINES

for Jane Hirshfield

make of it
in rounded plains, full speech
misunderstandings dissolved
in water carried, mountains formed